T0197203

# Lay Me Down Among the Words:

## A Collection of Poetry by a Trauma Survivor Whose Inner Voice Saved Her Life

By: Deborah Hallal Bradt, R.Y.T.
Cover by: Andrew Sykaluk

**BALBOA**.PRESS
A DIVISION OF HAY HOUSE

Balboa Press books may be ordered through booksellers or by contacting:

Balboa Press
A Division of Hay House
1663 Liberty Drive
Bloomington, IN 47403
www.balboapress.com
1 (877) 407-4847

Print information available on the last page.

ISBN: 978-1-9822-4662-4 (sc)
ISBN: 978-1-9822-4664-8 (hc)
ISBN: 978-1-9822-4663-1 (e)

Library of Congress Control Number: 2020907039

Balboa Press rev. date: 06/19/2020

"Don't let anyone steal your dreams,
not even yourself."

www.flyfreehealing.com

This book is dedicated to the amazing people at the Williams Skirball Writer's Center at the South Euclid-Lyndhurst Library. Special thanks to Dr. Mary E. Weems, Laurie Kincer.

Also, for Sally Ramsey, my amazing therapist, who helped me "carry the torch" when I wanted to end the race.

And for Jared West, my acupuncturist. Thank you for always believing in my capacity to heal.


In loving memory of my Daddy, David W. Hallal
1948-2004




You will always be my hero.
Thank you for guiding me every step of the way.
I miss you yet, somehow, I know you are still here, right by my side.

Love always,

Your "Angelface"

# Contents

# My First Poem: age 5
### *Sunrise*

As evening approaches,
how abstract is the sky,
full of vibrant colors
preparing to die.

Oranges and reds
intermingled as one,
striving to obtain
the setting of the sun.

# My Teenage Years:
## *Spirals 101*

I awake in Monet's waterlilies
staring into a sunflower's large brown pupil,
sweet and bitter.

Waters lap like mustache curls around me.

I grasp onto a lily pad,
float in perfect ellipses

away from my center.

Naked feet start to slip
but I catch myself.

I count how many spots cover a dalmatian
and lull through circles, black and deep.

I see through heavy spectacles,
spiraling lavender, flushed moments,

fly back to shore.

## Canvas Empty

Rosary beads sprinkle amethyst
like powdered sugar
across my nightstand,
stones, clear and hard,
bury an untouched cross.

I resist, massage each bead
between padded fingers,
listen to my breathing
and ponder away needless clutter.

Requests run through my mind
like a script
yet the words cling to my tongue,
as a foul odor in open air.
Like that book I stopped reading
where a faceless god seizes
my thoughts and paints abstract fantasies
on an empty canvas.

Now it sits with crumpled gum wrappers
on my nightstand,
one page folded over in invitation.

I shovel away the gravel
Heavy on my sanctuary,

flip open to the page,
read a sentence or two,

concentrate on inhaling fascinations,
shedding mindlessness,
counting little purple stones
and understanding why a half-empty can
of ginger ale
always goes flat.

# *Confession*

I often ponder the intricate
wrinkles of a raisin,
skin thin as Bible pages, worry
about the world
running short.

Through sunrise,
I calculate breakfast time,
shave twice in the shower
and arrive ten minutes
into morning's lecture.

When kleenex falls
from my baggy pocket,
I leave it crumpled
on the floor.

Smiles shout.

I forget to answer.

God invites me for lunch,
coats me like incense
warm in His blanket.

In an empty moment,
a plastic tray
and a deep, cleansing breath,

I accept.

I kneel down,
thank Him for the ease
of ten Hail Mary's
and rest in a bunch
of smooth red grapes.

## Low tide

When Sunday mornings drip
and stick to my skin
I stand in a niche
God carved
for my lanky toes,
as if in military position.

Sand hardens like day-old dough
as I press on.

It molds my feet.

Tiny granules cemented
into brown pavement
form a wide trail
crowded only by saturating breezes
that bounce off curled waves.

I hold a lollipop, melted purple,
And wonder how salt water
stings
shaven legs, heals
all wounds
and forms involuntary drops
out of dry eyes.

Pauses ebb with the current.

We meander into wordless worlds
ponder over status, business
suits and changing bodies
as crystals cling in between toes.

A turquoise sky washes us,
follows our feet.

Wisdom mingles in air
with the salt, saved
before it evaporates.

I find you.

Your chestnut hair,
your tanned body,
ageless and beautiful.

I hear your magnetic voice.

We walk in stride,
still caught in the niche,
traveling an expanded road,
listen to
sand solid
beneath us.

I wipe away grape candy,
hold on to your hand,

quenched by the orange day.

### *Spin Cycle*

my momma, in her brunette smile,
taught me how to measure detergent
so my cottoned whites didn't get stained

and how to learn from heroes.

daddy's pin-striped shirt was Superman's
as we flew, pressing our wrinkles like dough.

she sang while the washer overflowed
and I tasted bubbles popping
bitter
on my tongue.

I found creases and folded them
straight, stacking clothes like Legos,
called to daddy to keep them strong.

when I try to unload,
mom and dad approach me
in shadows murmuring stagnant words,

clinging to damp air like fabric softener.

I spot dad's cotton shirt crumpled
behind the dryer, lint heavy,
wearing green stains of mildew
and a tired gaze.

## *Paralanguage*

on mildewed nights, squeezed
hands and tight hugs
barely float.

I fold my fingers, cling
to a slender pen, meditate
through ink spots.

your crimson grin pangs
the pit of my stomach

in a sharp ache.

I rip through algaed,
rotten kisses, laugh
at our green lips

my chest pounds away
yesterday's interlocked
arms.

blue-green air cloaks
me, takes away
a brittle chill

I stare at freckled paper,
contemplate blotted words,
fill
pauses.

when I glanced over yesterday,
I spotted fear, circled it
and started over.

for tomorrow, splotched red ink
flows into a solid, smooth
line

bathed in night,
I glide with colored words,

praising unfilled pauses.

## The Train Station

air mixes with spiced cologne,
sour breath,
clings like musk to my crinkled suit.
a leather briefcase swims
in a puddle of dirt,
spilt cola, stale pretzels.
stiff and tall,
I choke on sighs
caught in still locomotion.
a hunched man passes
me, gripping a paper bag.

Buried treasure.

His face curled and sagging
like torn edges.

He pulls his head up
through sharp stubble,
and calls to me.

My gaze, fixed downward,
answers and I find
my briefcase, wrap dry fingers
around its metal handle.

His shadow follows me
as he limps away.

I pace with pointed heels,
stabbing the ground,

watch his train roar by.

## Chianti on the Rocks

The vintage year creases
Into dehydrated lines
Of thin, thirsty lips
And coats my throat hot.
At the tip of the crystal
Glass, gold water,
I catch your face floating,
As if dangling from a parachute,
Coming closer.
My fingers choke the rounded
Body of the cup, knuckles white,
Face wearing a delirious smile.
I inhale, breathing in the familiar -
Sips of blood-warm chianti
Thick steam of linguini
And your hand folded into mine
Like the teeth of a comb
Through knotted hair.
I scan the menu, wine list,
Find you reading
Me the same way.
Fascination lost in greasy
Napkins and words as dry as wine.
This chiseled place carved just for us
Cannot redeem that bloating heaviness
In my stomach.
I could have ordered chianti on the rocks
And stared at you
Through a frozen kaleidoscope
Yet I continue to sip heavy liquid
With a clear view
Of your disappearing smile.

## Catching Hilary

bony behinds pound into the see-saw,
bounce, one after the other,
sink into equilibrium
and skin forms bluish patches
like playdough.

laughter tangles in between
tree branches towards auburn petals
and I catch Hilary at the top,
keep her floating.
dandelion-yellow pigtails dance,
swallow sunshine,
encircle her head like a halo.
we sing recess,
engage in a pendulum's sway
until wood cracks
and see-saw's rhythm scatters
with fallen autumn leaves.

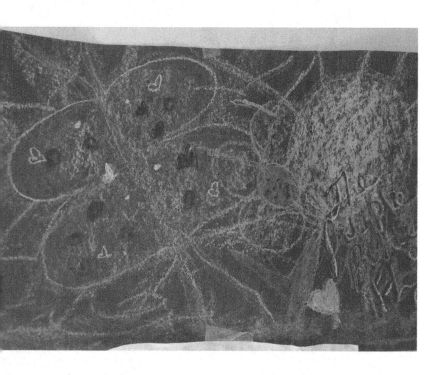

### *In Apogee*

a half-moon smiles
crosses your face
as if in equinox.
phases shift from
draped light
to molasses.
at solstice,
I chock on the speed
of time
and continue to rotate.
you remain at ease,
spinning around me,
cling to nothing
but whipped air.
I watch you
slip into apogee,
smile father and farther
away,
pray for an eclipse.

### *Finding Alpha*

Soldiers obeying
unspoken commands,
We pick them,
One by one,
Hold fern, baby's breath, carnation,
Watch as pot grows
And our flowers mesh
Into a patterned bouquet.

Our hands join like cotton candy
And we pray inside
The crisp night.
When humidity sprinkles
Rain I find it easy to be
Silent.

It helps that the flowers stand
Fresh, uncut, before us,
Our breath caught
In the beat of crickets
Constant as a windmill circling
In an August storm.

Doubts seep through
My pores into air
Cracking like fire.
I search into eyes,
Find my own reflections.
Our hands strum

The sign of the cross
And gems of rosary beads
Glide across our skin.
When our fingers untangle,
I let the breeze pass,
clothed in our knitted spirit.

## *Twilight*

I perch on a curved road
like an owl -
spread my wings for you,
taste gravel, exhaust,
your spiced cologne
and dripping salt
burning my lips.
the ashen sky
taunts me with its
small patches of blue.
I inhale, clasp my hands
together,
wander towards the end
of the curve.

You waver above me,
elevated, weightless,
once a solid man, wilted
as a dandelion plucked
form its root.
You fade like worn blue jeans -
hair pressed neat
glowing from sun-kissed face,
hazel eyes blink farther away.
wide smile stretches solid,
disappears into black
pavement leaving
me perched on this crooked
road with open,
bruised wings.

## *Lay Me Down*

I find my mother,
wrinkled and small
rippling away in a quick blue current,
taste a sweet gift from Bacchus.
I cast out my net, aim
for her diminishing body,
to lay in her heavy arms,
as she flies above the cedars of Lebanon.
Green hills surround her,
bury her within.
I stick to indented photographs,
Get caught between empty fragments,
unwritten words,
whirl into dreamscape.
She tip-toes over trees,
beckons me to soak
in her whisper.
My feet press into ground,
fling dirt as I run into brick-red
sky and dance alone.

# 2004- Present
## (The Awakening of My Poetry of the Soul)

# The Dance

*For: Daddy, I will always be your "Angelface"*

There is an empty space where I used to be.
Thoughts like shards of glass slice through my mind.
Black knots torment my gut.
The wandering, the restlessness,
Meandering through memories,
Clouded over with a soft hue.

Strip away sheaths,
Layer by Layer, Breath by breath.

No holding back now. No choice.

Now, I cry.

Again and again, I cry.

So much crashing forth, Like a wrecking ball, Across my life.

This empty space, It challenges me.

It beckons me to become undone.

I can't let you hold me.    I am not ready yet.

Play stay away.    Let me be.

When I danced in my room alone,

Soft curls bouncing under moonlight,
I didn't understand,

I only danced.

The noises. The thickness in the air.

Please, pick me up, Tell me it is all ok.

That I am OK.

Tell me it's not real. And then the page ripped,
Away, Gutted, Raw, Alone.

One fleeing, tightfisted
One stubborn second.

Unleashing blame.

And, so I dance again, humming to myself,
listen to my own voice, praying for a new day.
*~November 2007*

## *"The Miracle Tree"*

*Lola, my favorite writing partner*

Today I planted a new seed,
This seed is unlike any other I have ever planted.

It is simple, pure, effortless & tender.
It does not harm or ridicule.
It does not regret or judge.

This seed is unlike any other I have ever planted.

It feels its' wholeness in every moment
And does not question its' worth or strength.

It chooses to settle into the soil
And taste the sweet rain.

This seed is unlike any other I have ever planted.

It does not falter with the harshest of winters
Or wither when trapped inside a long drought.

It does not crumble within tsunamis
Or hurricanes,
Or pandemics.

This seed is unlike any other I have ever planted.

It takes it place in the
softest patches
of Green Earth.

It drops its' roots,
Impenetrable and steady
And expands with each passing moment
As it feels the sweet caress
Of Mother Earth &
Father Sky
Amidst the blazing sun

And kiss of the Solstice Moon.
This seed is unlike any other I have ever planted.

I watch as it sprouts,
Shooting Upward & Outward,
In every direction.

I watch as it dances & cries.

I watch its' magnificent leaves~
Its' blooms.
Its' buds.

I watch as it rests
Amongst the wonder of it all.
Softening, unraveling,
Shedding the unnecessary.

I breathe into it.
It breathes into me.

Expanding
Connecting
Dissolving....

Reclaiming

We are One.
*- July 4 2013, the veil has lifted*

# "The Purple Butterfly" Part I
## (in honor of those who struggle: In Loving Memory of Maureen A. & Lisa A.)

### *I am the Purple Butterfly~ Fluid and Free,*
### *And, even with broken wings, I will Fly again.*
*in gratitude for Highland Spring Hospital, Cleveland, Ohio*

Listless and beaten down, Worn and weary
Shattered- Locked in a vice grip,
Unable to move Or take a breath...

So different, So alone, Frightened,
So Misunderstood.

On an endless quest,
The poking and prodding,
Disapproval and Doubt,

Intense pressures- Empty promises...

Enduring bumpy roads, Holding on tightly,
Writhing, uncomfortable, Nowhere to turn...

So much confusion, Chaos
Contracting muscles, Insides churning,
Burning hot Collapsing into
An abyss...

Where am I? Who am I?
Pause...

Catch a glimpse of Deep blue sky,
Spacious and inviting-

Feel Earth Mother, Beneath my feet,
A gentle breeze, Washing through
Weakened bones And tired muscles,
Inviting me to soften...

Sense Spirit Cloaking me,
Holding me, Cradling me,

A warmth so sweet, So, nourishing-
Like nectar Pulsing through...

Healing deep wounding
Beneath gripped scar tissues, Inflammation,
Cooling years of heartache,
Melting through regrets.

Sense my eyes, Chocolatey brown
With flecks of gold, Echoes of my father,
Tears swelling- Falling gently down.

Caressing the beauty mark  On my left cheek,
The mark of my ancestry, That light up when I smile.

Sense my skin, Delicate and soft,
Chestnut hair flowing In the light breeze,

Tendrilled curls Cascading,
Like a halo, Around my shoulders.

Sense my core, The womb energy-
Unraveling, A gentle rocking inside.
Melting amidst the trees.

Feel steadiness beneath my feet As I Begin dancing on the
Plushness of green grass.

Feel my son- His sparking smiles
And tender spirit, Hug me from the inside.

Feel the rush- Unwavering love,
Of my husband Filling up the hollowness.

For my life…this life… Is not over.

I choose to live- To stand up
For who I am To reclaim my dignity-
To welcome this journey And let my inner yearnings
Finally awaken…

As a mother- As a wife- As a girl, As a lady, I AM ENOUGH.
*~October 2019*

## My Favorite Outfit
### Delilah

I wear armor most days.
It's my favorite outfit.

That way when you
look at me with those growling,
spitting eyes,

you can't see that my insides are crumpling.

This armor, it's silver and rusting, fits me perfectly,

I never leave home without it.

A tin can that camouflages
these knotted joints, constricted muscles
and bones that bristle as I take in a breath.

I wear it every day.

That way It shields me
from the razors of rage
and disappointment
that chase me incessantly,

until they leave me dangling
and grasping for air,
until they split
me open.

You think you know me.

It's funny because you
don't really see me.

So how do you possibly know me?

When you slapped me the other day
did you hear that

blood-curdling scream?
I like to muffle it.

That way when the heaviness
of your demeaning words
crush all twenty-six
of my vertebrae,

you don't have to see
me hunching over.

That way when my gut cramps
so much that I get dizzy and vomit,

I don't have to sense your laughter.

That way when I
Catch your chuckle.
As I trip and topple over
and my kneecap swells up
and ruptures.

That way when
my ankle joints wobble,
quiver and buckle

and when I finally collapse,

you don't have to see

I am weeping.

It's so much better that way.
*~February 2020, breaking the silence*

**"The Purple Butterfly II"**
*(in honor of those who struggle, in loving memory of Lisa & Maureen)*

Early this morning I saw her,
her fluttered wings
caught my eye,
it was a day I knew very well,
another day I wanted to die.

Lying crumpled on my pillow,
muscles gripped, blood so hot,
her orchid hue approached me,
a tiny, little dot.

Soon, I felt a pulsing,
it encompassed every cell,
her flecks of gold and lavender
made we want to yell.

I pulled up the covers,
digging deeper in my bed,
then I felt her lashes tickling
my forehead.

Her touch was first
a whisper,
my bones so
taut and tight,

then I felt her wings
enfolding me in light.

And so, the dance began,
rocking side by side,
she came and came again
and came again,

she wouldn't let me hide.

I thought I must be dreaming,
there was no way this could be.

This delicate,
purple butterfly
has set me free.
*~February 8, 1:08am*

## *The Bluebird's Song*

Today, I saw a bluebird
her wings spread wide and high,
she looked so sweet and delicate
it made me want to cry.

She danced upon the
autumn leaves,
spotting the oranges blue.

She spread her cheer
amongst fog and rain,
a joy I never knew.

She flew so high, so wide and free,
She never faltered or weakened~
She crested even the tallest oaks
yet her Light but only deepened.

Today, I saw a bluebird,
when all things seemed so lost,

When hearts were aching
And bones so tired
It seemed like an endless frost.

Yet there she flew
And flew some more

Upon cries and fears,
She began to soar ~

Thank you, Sweet Bird,
For your oceanic love,
For your long and soothing embrace.

Thank you, Sweet Bird,
For birthing me,
A song that will never erase.
### *During a winter storm & full moon,*
### *November 12th 2019*

### *The Invisible Heroes*

*Cork, Leah B. & Lisa C. & Fred, long- lost friends whose encouragement reignited the Teacher in me*

Those of you sinking
Into the four walls of your home,

Or driving, day and night,
Empty and alone.

Those who traverse bravely
Through sleet and snow.

Always ready and able,
Ready to go.

Those who sit by the bedside
As your loved one passes,

Feeling lost in the muck and the scattered,
Fallen ashes,
Hoping it will all come to an end.

Beloved Ones, It's not a matter of solitude, hiding or washing our hands, It's just a matter of being Born Once Again.
***-April 4, 2020***

# I Believe in Rainbows
### For Sally, In Gratitude

I believe in rainbows,
and the stars that smile
as night falls
and the moon that caresses
The sullen October skies.

I believe in rainbows,
in the midst of agony
when my bones ache
and muscles squeeze,
a harness encompassing
my humanity.

I still believe in rainbows,
radiant colors ever-flowing
after storms in winter,

Majestic indigos and purples,
Violets cascading across the sky,
As if dancing cheek to cheek.

Crimson, orange hues
catching morning dew
along with the butterflies
thirsting on their favorite blooms,
a nectar-filled delight

Amber yellows
that birth a halo upon
cumulus clouds
and torrential rains,
painting angel wings.

And then there's the blue,
Bold yet delicate
Turquoise-aqua, like the color
Of fresh pool water
Or the ocean at dawn.

Soon the arrival jade green
above barren trees
hollowed soil,
effervescent emeralds,
illumined and brave.

I believe in Rainbows
as I gaze now into thunderstorms
and heavy winds and fallen snow
and icicles,

As my knees melt into soft earth
And my weary eyes
Gaze upwards.

There is a glimmer in the sky~
It is there, I can sense it,

The rainbows are here,
They are floating into me.

The Bliss of the unknown
It wraps me like a Present,
Blanketing me, cozy and warm.

Thank you, rainbows,
Thank you

For cradling
and cloaking me,
for swaddling the darkness,
for your effervescent tenderness,
for your magic and your light,

for Being right here,
amidst it all,
for always believing in Me.
                *~ October 30, 2019 at dawn*

## "I Can Paint a Day"

*For: Malinda Z., my favorite unmet friend*

I can paint a day with hues of gold, violet
And the crispness of the winter dawn
Where I fall into the crevices of comfort
The sound of my son, laughing
The wind humming through dormant trees
Tingling in the tips of my toes
And a rhythmic heartbeat Steady and pure.

I can paint a moment within the landscape Of this pain
The burning, grip, shearing and tearing
The skin raw and weary
I hear her cries for tenderness
I feel her ache for breath
And I support her and let her widen
Soften, expand
And then contract again
I wipe her tears as she struggles
I cocoon her in light.

I can paint a path Winding and curious
With pebbles and stones With softness
And cement As I skip and dance
Swaying with the turns Floating with the soft sun
And sparkling aqua sky The sound of my feet
Like the rhythm of a drum Ever-flowing force
Will and delight.

I can paint away
all that pressed against my Truth
and diminished my words,
and the scars and the wounds,
all the fears and the fighting,
The pushing and pounding.

Today I paint anew I wait and I wonder,
curl into the unknown And let my colors fly.
**- Valentine's Day 2014**

# "Love"

*For: Bill (my soulmate, now and always)*

If my love was a liquid,
I would pour it into your body,
let it saturate you
cells, muscles, organs
and bones.
I would send it to the parts of you
that hurt the most.
Bathe them in a salve,

A soothing balm.

If my love was oxygen,
I would beg you
to take a breath.
And then another, until your lungs
spread
and widened
and you danced across the sky.

If my love was food,
I would fill it with nourishment.
It would be so sweet and tasty,
It would melt into you,
Until you had no choice, but to smile.

Maybe you don't feel it yet.
Close your eyes.
It's here.

The cup is on the nightstand.
It's filled with everything you need,

Now, go ahead, take a drink.
*- February 2, 2020 6:14am*

### *The Journey*
*Amineh, you will always be my soul sister*

Traveler,
I can see you must be lost
on this journey,
so crumpled and heavy,
shattered, torn apart.

I can see you huddled
there in the chasm,
hiding your whimpering
eyes into your
collapsed heart.

Traveler,
I can sense the crust
and crackling of your skin,
denied of moisture,
so bitter and dry.

I can sense that
guttural yell trapped
deep within you
pleading for a breath
every time you cry.

Traveler,
I can feel that clenching
That awakens you at 3am
when harshness and disappointment
slice you open.

I can feel the moistness
of your unshed tears
and all those words
you craved that were
never spoken.

Traveler, I notice you.
I see into your eyes
With their glints of gold
With sparks of jade
that twinkles
at their corners.

I sense the nectar
circling through your veins
as you lie in bed, awake,
along with all the mourners.

Traveler,
I hear that quiver
in your voice when you
reach your palm out
to catch mine.

Now, take a moment.
It will be ok.
Take it one step
at a time.

Traveler,
I promise, this time your way
Will be made clear,
Take hold of your map
and your pen.

It's time for you to pause
And to land right here.
You will never have to walk alone again.
*~February 2020*

# The Alchemist

*Andrew S., a friend whose kind heart, comforting*
*presence & amazing art helped me to shed the past for good*

I am a magician. Watch this.

Those stratus clouds,
saturated and heavy,
just turned into orchids,
lavenders and blushes,
smiling at me with a simple wave of my wand,

Just like that.

I am a scientist, watch this.

Sunken piles of mud and snow
now burst into beds of roses,
crimson and alive, catch the sheen
of afternoon sun,

Just like that.

I am an artist. watch this.

Within my inner landscape,
among sparks of nerves,
crackled bones, ravaged cells,
and exhaustion births two wings,
floating open as I shimmy and twirl
to syncopated rhythms upon
the empty canvas of
twilight's arrival,

just like that.

I am a physician, watch this.

Bruised, purpled skin and
gaping wounds now washed clean,
when even band aids can't stop fresh,

crimson blood from seeping.
Just like that.

I am a teacher, watch this.

Hollow, swollen joints
now glide with ease.
Twenty-six vertebrae
unraveling amidst this frigid, pale night,

just like that.

I am a magician,
watch this.

You told me I would never walk again, watch this.

Watch now.

Watch Me Fly.
*-February 2020, Claiming My Rebirth*

# *Joy Rising*

*Deanna B., the best bridesmaid and friend a girl could have asked for*

I can feel the Joy Rising!

It's rising in my soul.
It feels so amazing.
So out of control.

I feel it permeating,

In my muscles and my cells.

I feel these happy spaces,
Erupting weary yells.

I can feel the Joy Rising!
When it's dark and quiet.

I can feel the Joy Rising!
When all the world is silent.

*~April 6, 2020 12:31am*

## *Prayers for All Beings*
*Church of the Resurrection, Solon, Ohio*

"The War is Now Over.
Thank God Almighty,
We are FREE at last…"

Om Shanti…. Shanti…Shanti…

Peace to ourselves,
Peace to each other,
Peace to our earth,
Peace to all beings.

## *"How Can I Heal Today?"*

*Jessica & Master Roan*

How Can I Heal Today
When all Seems Lost and Broken?

How Can I Be Silent
With So Many Words Unspoken?

How Can I Gaze at Myself
When everyone else is scattered?

How Can I Be Free Again
When no one see how much they mattered?

*~April 7, 2020: 4:07am*

*Special Thanks to the Dao Temple
Mayfield Village, Ohio.
Especially for Irene & Kathleen*


*Our Invisible Heroes.*

# Prelude: Dear Mary

*Dr. Mary E. Weems, my favorite writing teacher, whose encouragement*
*saved my life*

I can only imagine
how your heart
must have broken open

the day you were struck by tragedy.

I can only imagine
that you may have some
unshed tears
and maybe even regrets,

I wish I could wipe them away.

I can only imagine
when you see a girl that
has the essence of your beauty
It might make your bones ache.

Dear Mary, if I could I would
fasten back together all the
lost pieces of your life

for there is no one
in this world I can think of that deserves
to feel a blanketing of love,
to have dreams fulfilled,
to be bathed in constellations,

no one that deserves a life
of inexplicable joy more than you.

Dear Mary,

You are a teacher who finds
a spark amidst the rubble of cataclysm.

I can only imagine
you may not always see
the gifts you bring every day

just by standing in front of me,
just from your kind eyes, just by being you.
                    **-February 20, 2020 12:13am**

## "The Dreamcatcher"

For: Terry Battaglia & The Church of the Resurrection
"Beautiful You" Retreat Team
In Gratitude

Have you left your dreams lingering
in the palm of your hand?

Are you crawling in the shadows
and not sure where to land?

Let your fingers gently open,
watch them float across the sky,

Let them catch a constellation,
you don't have to question why.

Let them curl down and flow
and whisper down your cheeks.

Standing firm on their puddles,
watch the sun as it peaks.

Let them soar above the clouds,
Let them fill you with delight.
Cradle them in your arms
until the world is filled with Light.

Amidst torrential rains
Heavy sleet and fallen snow,
let the wonder,
let the magic
let the joy begin to flow.

Land upon your precipice,
wherever you may be.
The Beautiful,
~You~
Set yourself free.

~January 2020, "Beautiful You Girl's Retreat" The Church
of the Resurrection ~ Solon, Ohio

# *"LOVE IS...."*

**A poem of Unconditional Love from a Blessed Momma to Her Son, Henry D.** ☺

*(For: Henry ~ You will always be my favorite boy and the sunshine in my heart!)*

*Love Is...*

*When you picked out those turquoise, pretty earrings for me last Christmas and they were heart-shaped too!*

*I love it when I put them on any time of day or night, even in my pj's, and they make me feel so beautiful!*

*That is because of you* ☺

*Love is....*

*When you turned to me in the car yesterday on the way home and said I bring "Sunshine into your life" ~*

*I love it when you know just what to say just when I need to hear it at just the perfect times!*

*How did you know I was about to cry that day??*

*Love Is...*

*When you come by my bed, any time of day and night, before school or after, or any time in between*

*When you look at me with those chocolate-brown eyes~*

*Oh, how I want to get my bathing suit on and take a swim in them!*

*Love Is...*

*When I see your face light up when we make biscuits and the entire house permeates with those amazing delights!*

*My favorite part of my day, dear Son, whether day or night, up or down, high or low,*

*Is when I hug you close to my heart and feel the warmth of your skin and sweet scent of you hair, right on your soft spot, at the top of your head.*

*Dear Son, Love is only Love when you are with me.*

*Thank you, Buddy, for being my one and only Favorite Boy.*

*Love always and Forever,*
*Your Momma*

***April 6, 2020, 5:12am, A New Day Has Begun***

## "Ectasia"

*Glasses, yes, they can be rose-colored.*

*Tainted.*

*The way you like to see them.*

*Well, you know.*

*Lately, when you look into my eyes, I see hollowness.*

*Unspoken words~*
*Tornadoes and torrents of brick and splatter dripping into*
*my skull.*

*Why all this heaviness?*

*I awoke this am, like clock-work*

*Right on cue.*

*It was 4:17am.*

*No alarm went off.*
*Just the shock and shivering of another nightmare.*

*The quaking inside*
*bones*
*crackled and fractured again*
*Under the summer's whisper.*

*That incessant hunger for*
*ecstasy.*

*An internal quivering of a heart*
*Broken open and unfolded again and again.*

*When you kissed me yesterday and caressed my silken skin,*
*did you mean it?*

*Or were you simply enjoying the "eye-candy" of a once infatuation?*

*You see, I am a lady.*

*I crave moments without thought or daily reminders of past mistakes.*

*Why is it so hard to breathe around you these days?*

*Dig up garbage and all you will get is more.*

*In the afternoon's hazy sky, I catch the stars and stripes out-side my window pane.*

*The eternal symbol of untethered freedom.*
*The United States of America.*
*A Free Country?*
*Maybe yes.  Maybe no.*
If that is the case, why do I whimper
and battle abdominal contractions most days still?
When was the last time you really looked into my eyes and saw me?


And what ever happened to the joy of being right here.


Together?


**~*June 16, 2020 3:56pm, lost in heartbreak***

# "THE COVID-19 CORONA CURE: CURE DEPRES-SION- CURE COVID-19"

### By; Deborah Hallal Bradt, RYT
### June 1, 2020

As I sit at my computer to type these words this morning, I am feeling quite ill.

Some of my current symptoms include the following:

Debilitating pain in my neck, hips, shoulders, back and knees, swollen joints, nausea, hay fever, chest tightness and heart palpitations, nightmares, loss of appetite, headache, anxiety/ worry and negative thoughts.

This is not something new for me.

I have had several of these symptoms in the past.

You see, I am a Trauma Survivor. I am also a Mother, Wife, Certified Yoga Teacher, Author and Holistic Health Coach.

The reason for me writing this article today, however, is not about me and all my symptoms.

It is about revealing TRUTH. As Martin Luther King Jr, declared, "Seek the truth and it will set you free...."

You see, what I have is actually not COVID-19. Although many of these symptoms sound similar to the virus.

What I have is another chronic illness that is also killing thousands of people around the globe.

It is called "Depression".

I also have another illness that not many people talk about in my regular health care visits.

That disease is called "Post Traumatic Stress Disorder".

These two diseases are not only real.

I believe they are at the heart of what is catapulting our globe and our precious city into flames as we speak.

The riots this past weekend in downtown Cleveland were another indication of my theory and that of many others of my friends around this city.

The more we separate. Isolate. Blame. Criticize.

The more we stay in hiding in our homes and walk around in our masks with our hands drying out from hand sanitizer, the more the deaths will continue to rise.

One statistic that I have noticed that is not being talked about much lately is that, during the course of the COVID-19 crises, not just in the United States, but around the world, children and adults alike are also dying of another disease.

That disease is called "Depression".

Depression is real. It isn't a made-up illness and it certainly doesn't get fixed from simply a pill or, even just a therapist.

In my opinion, what Is slowly killing our precious Mother Earth and our loved ones, like the late George Floyd (may he rest in peace), is undiagnosed emotional pain. Otherwise known as "Depression".

You see, the symptoms of depression are actually something all of us experience at one time or another in our lives but, for the sake of this article, I will simply point out the thoughts that often fill my head, especially when my fibromyalgia flares up.

Thoughts like, "It's all my fault. I will never be good enough. If I leave, my family will be better off. I can't take another day of this. I am burden on my husband. I am ruining my son's life... etc."

These thoughts come out of nowhere for me sometimes. They sprinkle through my brain like a passing Spring shower.

The problem is that, after many years of being bullied, judged, criticized, told I am less than other people and that there is no hope for my pain, these thoughts now mill though my mind on a daily basis.

Yesterday, I read an amazing article by Terry Pluto from the Plain Dealer that spurred me to finally speak out on the behalf of myself and my local community. His article was about adapting to change and, for me, the crux of the article was that we are all responsible for our choices.

That no one outside of us can "heal" us.

This is very true.

We, the people, have the power to heal ourselves.

For me, what is missing in our healthcare system, however, is a respect and dignity for those of us with Depression.

I have noticed that I get treated differently than other people when I go to a doctor appointment. Even if it is just for a physical.

They see I have a history of Depression and they seem to treat me differently.

I also noticed I get treated differently than my husband in many medical settings. For the sake of the urgency of this article, however, I will not go into details about this here.

Right now, we are in crises as a city, as a nation and as a globe.

This is not the time to accuse, judge or blame.

This is the time to UNITE.

To come together.

To stop all this right and wrong. Good and bad. Better or worse. Black or white. Etc. etc.

I think you get the idea.

I am a Middle Eastern-American.

Both my mother and father are Lebanese.

I am proud of my heritage and yet, at the same time, I find that I often hide who I am.

I also hide that I have a mental illness sometimes as there is such a stigma around it that I often don't tell my friends I want to cry myself to sleep many nights.

That all changed recently when I found an amazing organization called the Solon DBSA. The Solon DBSA is a brand of the Depression Bipolar Support Alliance (www.dbsa.org). They are a non-profit organization and they amazing things for so many people.

Our local chapter, held in Solon, literally saved my life.

It is time now for me to go and move forward with my daily responsibilities.

I have to find a way to put one foot after another. To get out of bed, even if I have only a few hours of sleep.

I am choosing to live. Even in the midst of all these thoughts and physical pain that bombard me on a daily basis.

That is my choice.

The bottom line is that the suicide rate since the COVID-19 crises has erupted is skyrocketing. I have attached a few stats above for you to refer to.

For me and my family, it is the social isolation and all this technology and lack of human connection that is making us feel sick more than anything.

The more we hide, isolate and separate, the more this globe as we know it will dissipate.

I, for one, enjoy watching the sun rising up over the evergreens outside my window. I love the feel of fresh, crisp air on my face and savor the nourishment of a deep breath.

Today, however, I can barely breath.

It isn't from COVID-19.

It is from heartbreak and sadness.

We must come together as a community before more people's health declines and more lives are lost.

For me, all of us are equal. All of us need the same things.

Shelter. Food. Friends. Family. Money.

Right now, however, I feel what we are missing most of all is connection and compassion.

For ourselves, especially.

So, I as finish this article, I plan to eat a nourishing breakfast and not just rush out the door and shame myself through my day today.

I plan to celebrate the beauty of the NOW moment.

Each moment is a gift, my friends.

Remember this. YOU are a gift.

Never give up hope, even if you have been told there is none.

Let's band together.

Let's rise up.

Before it's too late.

~June 1, 2020 8:07am

## "The Final Awakening"

*For: Master Lin & Master Roan*
*Two months after start of Corona-Virus Crises, Cleveland, Ohio*
*May 20, 2020*

After bowing and breakfast

All things are as they are today
And yesterday is now behind us.

The cock crowed this morning at 3am.
I answered her.

She was peeking up behind an evergreen tree and then
quickly fluttered away.
Then she morphed into a dragonfly.

Her right wing, clipped and dissipating...

Then she felt a breeze from the heavens
And the quiver of Mother Earth,
Her arms, warm and inviting-
Her soil, plush and pure.

All things are as they are today.
And yesterday is now behind us.

Down on my knees, feeling the hush of Jesus inside my
heart~
The tears of my soul poured through.

I answered her.

She was shining a light at the flecks of brown in my eyes.
She was showing me the locks of tendrilled curls
Cascaded over my weary shoulders,
Heavy with the burdens of the past.

Soon, a twinkle of sunlight glimmers it's morning song
upon me.
I gaze in the mirror at my face.

Tired, with bagged and swollen eyes.
Lips dry and crackling.

When I catch a glance of my face,
I see someone very familiar there~

But not me.

Her hair is a similar color.
Her face glowing and bright.

Different than mine, yet the same.

Soon, I felt a flutter.
I thought it might a valve issue with my heart.

Was I having chest pains?
Should I get to the hospital?

My body started trembling,
Shivering.

Crumbling
down.
Or so it seemed.

Then a hush filled my ears.
I even felt my brain quiet.

As an inhale entered my nostrils….my lungs slowly filling
the hardened spaces of years past.

Soft earth became firmer and more palatable beneath my
tired, curled toes.

I gazed again at my reflection.
Heard the cock crow again.

This time the song so lyrical and sweet.

I saw myself.
I saw You.

I saw my Mother in my own eyes.

We hugged together this morning in the mirror.

And, as I turned to walk away, I saw a squirrel dancing up
the wild oaks in my backyard.

There was a fresh gust of air penetrating the wilderness.

And, so mother and daughter cradled one another into the
sunset.

A new day has begun.

*~ May 20, 2020 8:44am*

# "Dancing"
*For: Me, In Gratitude*

I noticed this morning the sound of the wind howling madly through the trees outside my window

And so, I was dancing

I was dancing with thoughts in my head about who might be seeing me up at 3am. Lights on in my home. Belly constricted.

The hush of God permeating throughout my beingness and yet also the Essence and reminders of the shame and pain underneath everything.

How many years will I have to continue to prove my worth? To prove I am enough? To you or anyone.

How many more solitary moments will I have to spend exhausting my energies on this endless quest of validation?

I ask you this. How many? How long? How much?

Will this ever end?

As I gaze around my writing and yoga space, my eyes dart from little hints of beauty around me. Light flickering lavender beams from one of my latest paintings (which no one yet has seen since I hide most everything).

I see glimmers of butterflies dancing and cascades of rainbows.

Hues of crimsons, reds, oranges, peony pinks, glorious golds and the essence of aqua and waterfalls.

And yet all I feel is the squeezing and the gripping and utter exhaustion of this moment.

The joy is in the background.

The pain is so here and present. The ache that strangulates me most nights and days, basically hourly.

And so I yearn to dance. To put on my tap shoes. My purple tutu, especially when the sun shines as that is when it sparkles the brightest.

I so yearn to have a gigantic dance floor right here before me instead of all this clutter and chaos.

I ask you, why not now?

Why not put on my dancing shoes? My feet may be swollen. My eyes sagging and wrinkled.

But I can still dance, my friends, I can still dance!

And so my body starts it's syncopated rhythms. Side to side, front to back. All directions.... going wherever it wishes and dreams to go.

And so, I am dancing.

Dancing amongst the whirling winds, chilled caresses of the Springtime moons.

I am dancing among the castles and the museums in my mind, so crystal and clear.

I dance with my heart and the rose blossoms that blink from inside it when my son whispers the word "Momma" and wraps me in his loving arms.

I dance when I smell his hair. When I feel his heart beating with me.

And so we are dancing.

Dear Ones, please remember to put on your dancing shoes.

Right now,

Before it's too late.

*~May 6, 2020 3:25am,*

# "We Are United"

*By: Deb Bradt, RYT, March 12, 2020*
*This Poem is Dedicated to: All Beings, Near and Far*

*In the midst of chaos and struggle,*
*We are United.*

*In the midst of trauma and stress,*
*We are United.*

*In the midst of heavy shadows*
*and shattered hearts,*
*We are United.*

*The time is upon us.*
*The time is now.*

*All of us have*
*what it takes*
*right now,*
*to look within*
*and see the Truth.*

*We are United.*
*We are One.*
*There is nothing*
*we can't handle*
*together.*

*There is nothing more to fear.*

*In the midst of these gray skies,*
*and crippling pain,*
*The puffed cumulus clouds*
*Of Spring*
*are arriving.*

*The daffodils, yellowed and bright,*
*are cresting through*
*earth's tender soil.*

*Patches of aqua dance*
*sweetly*
*with the bluebirds*
*across our skies.*

*No matter who you are,*
*No matter how badly*
*you hurt,*

*Remember, we are united,*

*Together forever.*

*We are One.*


*We are United.*

*We are Free.*


*~May 24, 2020*

# "Is It Ever Really Quiet Time?"

*By: Deb Bradt, RYT*

*February 16, 2020*

I woke up last October in a daze. The fluorescent lights flickering of our room kept flickering which didn't help my throbbing headache. My head pounded so much I could barely lift it up off my pillow. Then a screeching voice crackled through the loud speaker near the head of my bed, startling me. My stomach muscles tightened as I heard the announcement, *"It's 3pm. Time for 'quiet time'. Sixty minutes. Stay in your rooms. Lights out."*

Every day at this time we are told to take "quiet time". At this time of the afternoon on our unit, it was supposedly time for us to relax. There were no activities or groups planned. Dinner wasn't until 5pm.

For me, it felt more like torture.

My roommate seemed somewhat comfortable with the idea. She got out her journal and starting jotting a few things down. A few minutes later, I knew she must be eating something. I could smell the stench of her leftovers from lunch. She kept sneaking food into our room.

Me, on the other hand, I felt lost. Constricted. Confused.

I wanted so badly to rest. I tried and tried. My hospital bed felt more like laying on bricks than a mattress. I twisted and turned to get into any position that was remotely comfortable. It was practically impossible to find a position I could stay in for more than a few moments. It was bad enough pretending to be relaxed.

I yearned to feel human again. At home the night before, I had hit such a low point, I literally wanted to jump out of my bedroom window. My life had become a robotic nightmare. I wasn't really living. I was only pretending to. It was like living in a strait jacket. The crushing pain in my body exhausted me. It wasn't just headaches and lower back pain. I started to have what seemed like heart problems too as well. Palpations. Chest pain. Nausea too.

I had been to the ER several times in the past few weeks to get checked for a possible heart attack.

The EKG was normal every time.

*This is normal?*

I hadn't slept for weeks. Months even. Every time I tried to lay down, my body trembled and twitched. I was on overdrive 24 hours a day. I felt all knotted up. I hadn't eaten a full meal in days and had lost at least 10 pounds months in the past month.

I didn't even enjoy hugging my son anymore.

When I was at my doctor yesterday for my annual checkup yesterday, something I said must have alerted her office. It must have slipped out somehow that I felt hopeless. That I wanted it all to be over. I don't remember saying anything like that and wish I would have kept my mouth shut.

I heard her staff mumbling things like, "suicidal ideation" and "psychiatric emergency" to each other.

I thought, *"What does "suicidal ideation" really mean? That I am so miserable, I want to die? Ok, I am. Now what? What are they going to do about it?"*

Then someone said, "call 911."

I heard them tell my husband, *"The ambulance is on the way, Mr. Bradt. We have to get your wife to the closest ER asap. She is not allowed to go home."*

Those words hit me so hard, I almost fell over. It seemed as if the walls of the room I was in started to close in on me.

I was trapped. They were going to take to me the ER and God only knows where I will be sent after that.

*How many times do I have to go through this?* I hate ambulances. Their screaming sirens scare me, not to mention the bumps and bright lights. I had been in and out of that emergency room so many times that year that the staff there knew me by first name. They would glare at me as I was being wheeled in or roll their eyes as if to say, *"what is she doing her again?"*

There was nowhere to turn. Nowhere that felt like home, at least. Here I was again on my way to another hospital. Nine times in the past twelve years. *How many more times would I have to go through this? Is this all I have to look forward to for the rest of my life?*

It felt like my life was a cd with a huge scratch across it that kept skipping to the same section. Rants of incessant thoughts bombarded me constantly. Thoughts like *"You messed up again. You are such a disgrace. You can't do anything right. It's all your fault".* An endless tape recorder ran through my mind with no "pause" button.

It was like being bullied by my own brain.

*Will I ever feel human again? What about my son? How is he? He must be so scared. What am I going to do?*

I ended up a hospital I hadn't been to before. On the east side of town. On this particular unit, they had "quiet time" daily. This was something new for me. Normally, I like the quiet. These days, thought, I didn't like much of anything.

About forty minutes into "quiet time" on that October particular afternoon, I heard a shuffling at my door. Two medical assistants busted into my room. One grabbed my arm and said, *"time for bloodwork, Deborah. Roll onto your side".* I prefer "Deb" but I kept that information to myself. There was no time to catch my breath before I felt the needle go in. A jolt of sheering pain tore through my body. My head began pounding again. They left in a hurry. On to the next room.

I couldn't say a word. Trembling, I looked at my watch.

Fifteen more minutes of quiet time.

Moments later I heard a man's voice reverberated through the unit. It felt as if I was in the middle of a battlefield. I heard pounding. It felt like it was right outside my door. He was yelling expletives to another patient. The seething anger in his voice cut through me. My body trembled as I got into a fetal position, covering my ears and squeezing my eyes shut.

*How was I supposed to rest with all this chaos? Will this ever end?*

I wanted everything to disappear, including me. A few moments passed. And then a few more. I continued to lie there, hoping I would somehow become smaller and smaller and eventually fade away.

Then something prompted me to open my eyes. Still curled up on the bed, I caught a glance of the window in our room. The rusted, vertical blinds were open just enough. I could see a hint of white and then blue. Even though, I still heard clattering in the background, that patch of color seemed to become larger.

I walked over to the window.

I spotted a flock of birds. They were blackbirds. Their wings were spread and they looked as if they were floating. Then a glimmer of sunlight peaked out. I could almost feel a bit of warmth across my face, as if the sun was shining on me.

I became mesmerized by this scene.

The vibrancy of the fall colors mixed with the majestic birds and afternoon light. Hues of crimson, gold and orange glistening through our hospital room window. A tapestry of wonder.

My toes and fingers started to wiggle a bit as I continued to gaze into the Autumn Sky.

Then, there was a knock at my door. It was gentle and soft. Almost like a whisper.

*"Hi Deb. Just coming to check on you. Are you alright?"* she asked.

It was my nurse, Jennika. I recognized her voice. She was now standing behind me, waiting patiently. She placed her hand on my upper back. My shoulders softened a bit.

*"It's ok, Deb. It's all ok"* she said.

I slowly turned around. I wanted to look her in the eyes.

*It's all ok, Deb",* she repeated.

The room became still. Her hazel eyes met mine.

It was finally quiet time.

### *"The Warriors of Hope"*
*By: Deb Bradt, RYT*
*In Honor of Rebirth, March 16, 2020*

*A cataclysmic shift*
*is upon us.*
*We can no longer*
*run or hide.*

*The tides are turning,*
*gravel crumbling,*
*we must rise up*
*and abide.*

*Let's delve into*
*forgotten worlds*
*under our sullen,*
*downcast eyes.*

*Drop into this*
*withering earth,*
*exhale until the*
*emptiness dies.*

*Although you think*
*you walk alone,*
*all you need is to*
*broaden your scope.*

*Standing right behind*
*you and all around*
*soar flocks of angels*
*and Warriors of Hope.*

*When the gravel*
*beneath your soiled*
*shoes start to churn*
*and seems to weaken.*

*You need look no*
*further than where*
*you stand and soon*
*the links will deepen.*

*For broken wounds*
*and untouched hearts*
*no longer have*
*a place to land.*

*For We, together,*
*are the Warriors of Hope*
*And forever*
*we will stand.*

# "Can We Rise Up?"

**For: The Late and Beloved George Floyd,
You Are A Hero for Us All, In Gratitude**

*Searching and wandering,
aimlessly,
longing for a way out*

*Or,*

*at least a small flickering
of candlelight in
this deep emptiness of this
muck-filled abyss*

*we call home.*

*Can We Rise Up?*

*Then, the stars that flicker
and wink through thunder
and rain in the deep
night*

*start calling.*

*Can We Rise Up?*

*As they peek
through crusted lands,
thick fog, rumbling,
misty rains
and heavy currents*

*of fear and agony.*

*Can We Rise Up?*

*For this night, Dear Ones,
deep within our*

*very Beings, lies a pattering,*
*A Crying Out,*

*A Pleading to be held*
*and cradled and*
*lavished under this*

*Sweet, Springtime Moon.*
*Let us rise up.*

*Let us soak in the sounds*
*and the soft cries*
*that sing*
*and hum*
*in the darkest,*
*deepest spaces of*

*Our Weary Hearts.*

*Let us rise up.*

*Let us listen intently*

*To the hushed voices*
*that dance wildly*
*in the hidden mystery*
*and barren Oaks*
*on this still, quivering night.*

*Let us rise up.*

*The music that soars*
*above the evergreens,*
*and wanders beyond*

*The Crackling of our Souls.*

*It is time now, Dear Ones,*
*for Us to*
*Rise Up.*

*As our eyes gently*
*Open*
*And the flickering stars*

*Light Our Way*

*And We Fly Free,*

*Together,*

*Bathing in the wonder*

*Of It All.*


*~March 30, 2020*
*A New Day Has Dawned*

*And to my unwavering Faith.*
*Thank You.*

*And So It Is.*

## About the Author

Deborah Bradt has been fascinated by words since she was old enough to hold a crayon. She began her poetic experiments first as a very young girl as her word explorations helped her to vent her deep-seated feeling of shame and loss that she could never seem to shake off. You see, Deborah was born in a traditional hospital setting. At the time of her birth, her parents were married. However, soon after she was born, her parents ended up getting a divorce. Although Deborah was a very young child, she still remembers feeling broken open by this experience of moving away from her father, David. W. Hallal. Although she lived a "charmed life" in Central Florida and had many material goods, she never truly felt safe and at ease in her body or in her life. She experienced much abuse in her life including sexual, verbal and physical abuse. She tried to take her own life several times, feeling that much of the hatred she felt from others was her fault. Creative self-expression and poetry, in particular, however, became Deb's best friend. Even as a small child, she would recite poetry in the middle of the night when she awoke from nightmares or when she had to leave home just to get away. Her words kept her going, through the darkest of times. Honestly, she does not think she would have been here on this planet at age 47 if she had not discovered her gift of playing with words. She ended up graduating from Florida State University in Interpersonal Communications with a minor in Creative Writing in 1993 and has never had a moment of her life since without a pen in her hand.. Deb is deeply and profoundly grateful to all those who supported this book project and Balboa Press for all their patience in getting this book published. It is literally a dream come true. Namaste.-Deborah Bradt, R.Y.T.

Printed in the United States
By Bookmasters